the Real Housewives OF NEW YORK CITY

COLORING BOOK

BY @DRUNKDRAWN

"You don't support other women!"
- Ramona

Queen Morgan relaxes in bed.

"I'll tell ya how I'm doing, not well bitch!"
- Dorinda

"Are you kidding me, Bethenny?!"
- Ramona

"Please don't let it be about Tom."
- Luann

"Clip!"
- Dorinda

"I cooked. I decorated. I made it nice!"
- Dorinda

Ramona in quarantine enjoying a glass of red wine and a face mask.

Bethenny sreams.

Carole listing all of Bethenny's insults.

"The hostess with the mostest!"
- Dorinda

Season 11.

Bethenny's Miami meltdown.

Jill hits the ice.

"She was trying to kill me!"
- Kelly

the Real Housewives
OF NEW YORK CITY

Season 1.

Season 1.

Season 1.

Season 1.

Season 1.

Season 1.

"*I can't. I can't. I can't!*"
- Ramona

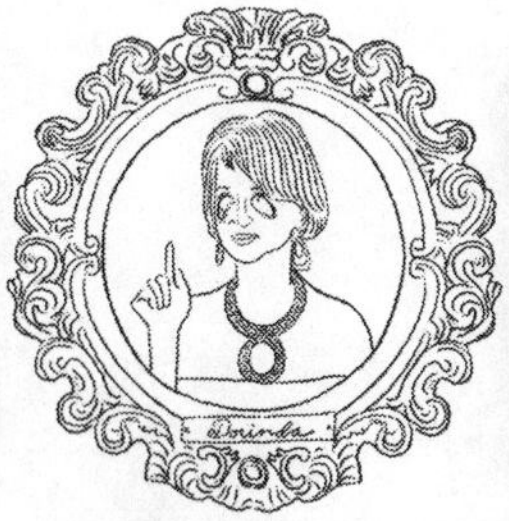

MONEY TALKS

WEALTH WHISPERS

"Get the pinot grigio!"
- Alex

"You're both white trash, quite frankly."
- Aviva

Luann sits down with Andy to discuss her arrest.

"What are you doing here with Dorinda?!"
- Sonja

"Pecuuuuuliar."
- Ramona

"Focus. Focus. Focus."
- Dorinda

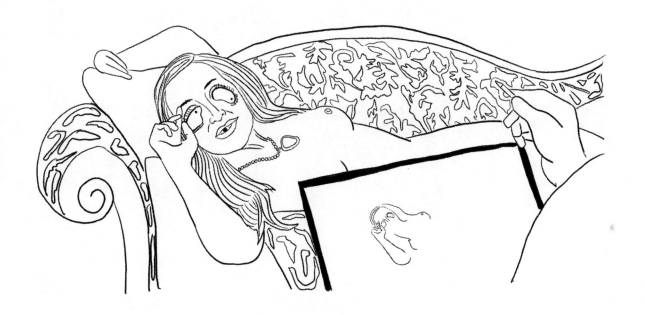

"Draw me like one of your French girls."
- Sonja

GHOSTBUSTERS

Bethenny and Carole go at it.

"Here's to those who wish us well and those who don't can go fuck themselves."
- Bobby Zarin

"She's a slob kebab."
- Dorinda

Luann as Diana Ross.

Carole's last summer.

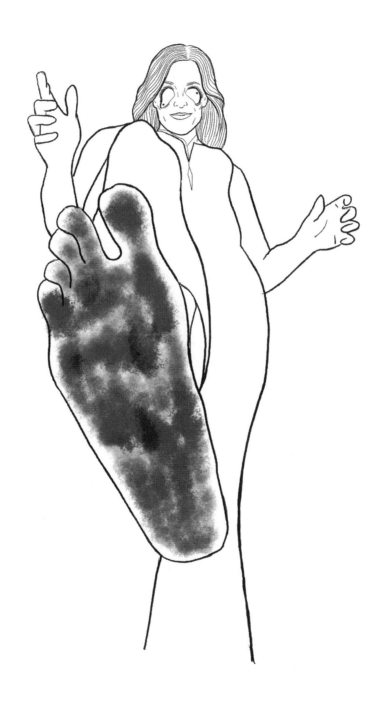

Luann leaves the "ultimate gift".

"Wow! Bethenny, wow!"
- Ramona

"Chobani!"
- Dorinda

Barbara the bisexual.

Jill with a portrait of Ginger.

"Jovani!"
- Dorinda

Sonja with a lime in her mouth.

The Singer stinger.

The infamous Rey.

"She looked like an alien invaded her body."
- Jill

Sonja naked wasted in the pool.

"I broke my tooth!"
- Sonja

"Where are the hot guys?!"
- Bethenny

Christmas in the Berzerkshires.

Dale!

Doorobics.

Harry and Ramona.

"Carole, I could give you your first squirting orgasm."
- Aviva's father

"My babies!"
- Tinsley

"You look like the joker."
- Bethenny

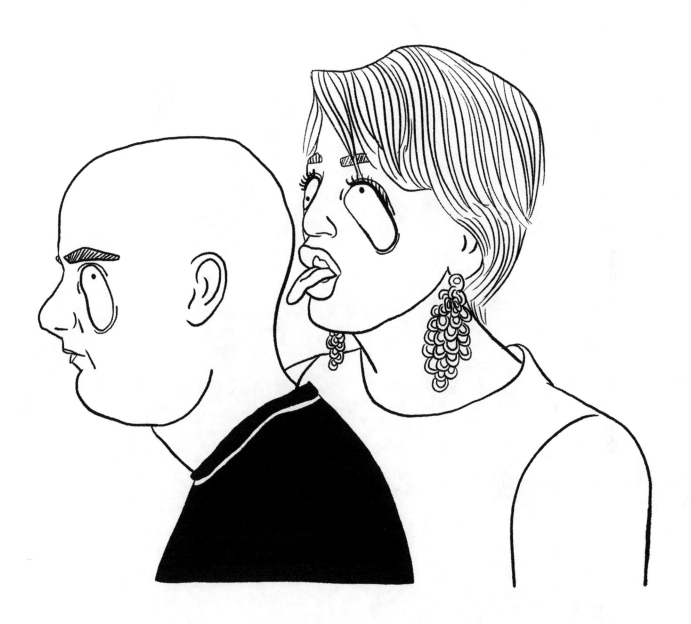

"I love a bald man."
- Dorinda

"Take a Xanax! Calm down!"
- Ramona

"Be cool. Don't be all uncool."
- Luann

"You know what, Bethenny? We are done."
- Jill

"Go to sleep. GO TO SLEEP!"
- Bethenny

ABOUT @DRUNKDRAWN

Ryan Casey created **Instagram.com/drunkdrawn** in the Spring of 2017 after finding some sketches he did while drinking, drawing and watching *The Real Housewives*. Ryan is an author, illustrator and designer. He has created art for Broadway.com, Rolling Stone, Us Weekly, Bravo, Vanity Fair, Twitter, Buzzfeed, The Grammys, The Billboard Music Awards, The American Music Awards, HBO, Bravo's *Watch What Happens Live!*, The Wall Street Journal, The Huffington Post, Marc Jacobs, and Urban Outfitters.

@GoRyanGo
GoRyanGo.art

Thank you for your support.
Cheers!

Made in United States
Troutdale, OR
09/20/2023

13054873R00066